Keeping Unusual Pets

COCKATIELS

Belinda Ogle

Heinemann
LIBRARY

www.heinemann.co.uk/library

To order:
☎ Phone 44 (0) 1865 888066
🖹 Send a fax to 44 (0) 1865 314091
💻 Visit the Heinemann bookshop at www.heinemann.co.uk/library to browse our catalogue and order online.

First published in Great Britain by Heinemann Library, Halley Court, Jordan Hill, Oxford OX2 8EJ, part of Harcourt Education.
Heinemann is a registered trademark of Harcourt Education Ltd.

Editorial: Nancy Dickmann and Tanvi Rai
Design: Ron Kamen and Celia Floyd
Picture Research: Rebecca Sodergren, Catherine Bevan and Liz Eddison
Production: Séverine Ribierre

Originated by Dot Gradations
Printed in China by WKT Company Limited

ISBN 0 431 12415 9
08 07 06 05 04
10 9 8 7 6 5 4 3 2 1

British Library Cataloguing in Publication Data

Ogle, Belinda
Cockatiels – (Keeping Unusual pets)
636.6'8656

A full catalogue record for this book is available from the British Library.

Acknowledgements

The Publishers would like to thank the following for permission to reproduce photographs:

Ardea/D & M Trounson: p. 16 (top); Ardea/Jean-Paul Ferrero: p. 9 (top); Ardea/John Daniels: p. 6 (top); Corbis/Eric and David Hosking: p. 7; FLPA: p. 8; FLPA/J&P Wegner: p. 18; Maria Joannou: p. 43; NHPA/Ernie Janes: pp. 17, 6 (bottom); Oxford Scientific Films/Steve Turner: p. 5; Oxford Scientific Films/Austin J Stevens: p. 9 (bottom); Tudor Photography: pp. 10, 11 (top), 11 (bottom), 12, 13, 14, 15 (top), 15 (bottom), 16 (bottom), 19, 20, 21 (top), 21 (bottom), 22, 23 (top), 23 (bottom), 24, 25 (top), 25 (bottom), 26, 27 (top), 27 (bottom), 28, 29 (top), 29 (bottom), 30, 31, 32, 33 (top), 33 (bottom), 34, 35, 36 (top), 36 (bottom), 37, 38, 39 (top), 39 (bottom), 40, 41 (top), 41 (bottom), 44, 45 (top), 45 (bottom).

Cover photograph of the cockatiel, reproduced with permission of Tudor Photography.

Disclaimer

Contents

Any words appearing in the text in bold, **like this**, are explained in the Glossary.

What is a cockatiel?

If you are reading this book then probably either you or someone that you know is thinking about owning a cockatiel. Not only are you considering a great pet, but you have also made a very sensible start by trying to find out as much as you can about cockatiels before you make your final decision. Far too many people buy new pets without much idea about how to look after them, which only ends up making both the owner and the new pet very unhappy.

Cockatiels are from the group of birds called parrots, which mean that they are closely related to cockatoos, budgies and macaws. They are probably one of the best pets that you can choose and are particularly good for children or young adults. They are relatively easy to look after and if you give them plenty of love and attention, and the care that they need, they can live for around 14 years.

A handsome bird showing off the crest of feathers on its head.

Where do they come from?

In the wild cockatiels are very common in Australia where they can be seen flying in many gardens or looking for food at the edge of roadsides. They are a fairly small bird in comparison to the macaws and larger parrots, only growing to a length of around 28 centimetres, including their long tail.

These birds are rose-breasted cockatoos. They are closely related to cockatiels.

Why are they called cockatiels?

The name 'cockatiel' comes from the **Portuguese** word 'cacathitho' which means 'little cockatoo'.

Special feet

Cockatiels and all parrots have very unusual feet for birds. Normally birds will have three toes pointing forwards and one pointing back. Cockatiels and other parrots, however, have two toes pointing forward and two pointing backwards. This enables them to pick up their food and hold it while they eat, which is particularly common among the larger parrots, though less so with cockatiels.

5

Colours and markings

Cockatiels are beautiful birds, with a crest of feathers on the top of their head. They come in a variety of different colours and colour patterns, but don't come in the bright colours that you see in budgies and macaws.

Whatever cockatiel colour you choose it will always be made up of black, red, white and yellow. It may have all of these colours or just one or two; some may have very strong colour or others very pale. Occasionally you will find one with no colour at all. This is called an **albino**. There are a few common colour varieties.

Many cockatiels have orange cheeks.

Here are two normal grey cockatiels and a Lutino cockatiel perched on a branch. Notice how their toes clasp around the branch.

Some varieties of cockatiel:

- 'Pied' cockatiels are blotchy looking with white and yellow patches.
- 'Pearled' varieties have white or yellow feathers, and each feather has a grey edge.
- 'Lutino' birds don't have any black colouring so appear as a pale yellow.
- The 'grey' or 'normal' colouring is probably most commonly seen. The bird will have a mainly grey body with a yellow head and white bands on the wings.

Pets are a big responsibility

As with any animal, once you take on the responsibility of owning a pet, you are completely responsible for its care and its behaviour. So, you need to decide if you really can provide all the care that your new pet needs.

You will have to spend time with your pet every day and attend to its needs. If you think that it may be ill, you should always get a vet to check it out.

Cockatiels are intelligent and sociable birds. Because of their high intelligence they need mental stimulation from you and their environment.

Your responsibilities:

- Never buy a pet without first considering the good as well as the bad points.
- Never buy a pet because you feel sorry for it.
- Young children are not allowed to buy pets. Take an adult with you when you go to buy your cockatiel.
- Once you own a pet it is your duty to care for it, so you need to decide if you really can.
- If your pet is ill you need to take it to the vet, so make sure you know a good vet before you buy your cockatiel.

Cockatiels in the wild

When thinking about owning a pet it is often a good idea to find out how they live naturally in the wild, so that you can understand the best way to look after them as a pet.

Where do they live?

Cockatiels live in the wild in Australia, particularly in the middle of the country that is very hot and dry. They like to make their nests in the **hollows** of trees and will try to find trees that are near water so that they don't have to travel far to get a drink. They will normally nest 2–8 metres off the ground depending on where the suitable hollows are in the tree.

This group of cockatiel chicks have just hatched out of their eggs. Both cockatiel parents prepare the nest hollow, nurture the eggs and care for their young.

Cockatiels in the wild live in large groups travelling from one feeding place to another.

How do they feed?

Cockatiels normally look for their food on the ground, where they eat various grass seeds, as well as shoots and buds of different plants. If they are eating on the ground and are frightened by a **predator**, cockatiels will fly up into the branches of the trees. So, if your pet cockatiel becomes scared it will automatically fly upwards.

Who do they live with?

Cockatiels are sociable birds and live in large flocks. In the wild they have to constantly keep moving in search of water, so it is safer and easier to do this in a large group. They whistle to alert other flock members of danger, food or their location. Their pale colourings help to **camouflage** them from predators.

Wild parrots, like these pink cockatoos, eat seeds, leaves, bark, fruit and berries.

Is a cockatiel for you?

It is very important to choose a pet that suits your way of life and your daily routine, and one that will provide you with all the things that you want from it. Otherwise you will soon get bored and neither you nor your new pet will be happy.

A cockatiel is an ideal first pet. They are incredibly friendly and intelligent birds that respond well to human contact. They are not very expensive or difficult to look after and they make an excellent pet. But before you make up your mind, here are some points that you should consider.

Are they good with other pets?

Birds and cats do not get on well together, so if you have a cat it's probably best not to buy a cockatiel. Dogs are not as bad, as long as the cage is well out of the dog's way, and the cockatiel is not let out of its cage when the dog is about. Other pets such as **rodents**, rabbits and other birds should all be able to live in peace together as long as they are all housed separately.

Having two pets can be twice as much fun, as long as you get the right combination!

Can I tame a cockatiel?

Cockatiels are very intelligent and will very quickly learn to come and sit on your finger, do tricks and can even be taught to repeat the odd word or two. Cockatiels are not such good 'talkers' as some of the larger parrots or even budgies, but with a lot of patience they can learn a few words. The more time you are prepared to spend with your cockatiel, the **tamer** it will become.

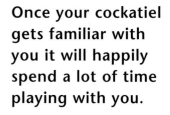

How much space does a cockatiel need?

Cockatiels need to be able to fly and stretch their wings. A normal budgie cage is not big enough for a cockatiel. The cage should not be less than 60 cm × 60 cm × 90 cm for a single bird.

Once your cockatiel gets familiar with you it will happily spend a lot of time playing with you.

The main thing to remember when it comes to choosing a cage for your cockatiel is to get the biggest one that you can afford and have room for.

A big commitment

Any animal is a big commitment and you need to make sure that you will be able to give it all the care and attention that it needs. A cockatiel will take at least 15 minutes a day to look after, and could live for over 14 years. Can you commit to that amount of time every single day for the rest of its life?

Holidays

You also need to think about who will look after your pet if you go on holiday. It will have to be someone you can trust completely and would be willing to help out.

Lots of attention

Other than food and water the most important thing that you need to give your cockatiel is attention. They need far more company and **stimulation** than other birds. If they don't get all the attention that they need they can suffer from a number of illnesses and complaints, and even death, as a result of their boredom.

If you are out a lot, maybe you should consider getting two birds. That way, although they will still need attention from you, they will at least have a friend for company if you are out.

This bird is cleaning its feathers. This is a healthy habit and cockatiels spend a lot of time doing it.

Cockatiel good points:

- They are easy to tame.
- They are quite cheap to look after in comparison to dogs and cats.
- They are very friendly and intelligent, so they can learn tricks easily.
- They are attractive to look at and fun to watch.
- They don't get ill very often.

You will need to clean the floor around and under the cage every day to get rid of droppings and scattered seeds.

Cockatiel not-so-good points:

- They need a lot of attention to stop them becoming bored.
- They need a lot of space. A nice big cage can be quite expensive to buy, and takes up a lot of room.
- A **hand-reared** bird can be quite expensive to buy.
- You will need someone to look after them when you go away.

Choosing a cockatiel

Firstly you need to think about how many birds you want to keep. A single bird is often thought to become **tamer** than a pair as it will soon consider itself as part of the human family. However, a single bird will need a lot more time and attention to prevent it from getting bored. If you think that your new pet will have to be left on its own for several hours a day, then you should consider getting two birds.

The other option is to keep an **aviary**. This allows the birds to behave in a way that is similar to how they would live in the wild, and allows you to keep several at a time. Aviaries will also offer the birds much more space. Aviary birds are not as likely to become as tame as single birds or a pair. If this is the first time that you have kept a cockatiel or any birds, it's probably best to get used to keeping just one or a pair before you start to think about a whole aviary full.

If you keep many species of birds, make sure that they are suited to living in the same aviary.

Getting ready

You must get the cage and all the necessary equipment, including food, before you purchase your bird. The stress of being moved will upset the bird, so it needs to be placed quickly in its new cage and environment.

Pet shop or breeder?

There are good points and bad points about buying your new cockatiel from both pet shops and breeders. Some pet shops may offer a written **guarantee**, so if your new pet doesn't seem to be very healthy despite taking it to the vet, you can return it and get your money back. Breeders are less likely to do this.

Breeders, however, have a lot more experience of **rearing** and caring for cockatiels and can often offer advice whenever you need it throughout your bird's life. Breeders will also normally offer **hand-reared** birds which, although more expensive, will ultimately become tamer, more friendly pets. Birds purchased from good breeders will normally have been less exposed to disease so they are often healthier. They will also not have had to experience the stress of being moved to a pet shop, or the noise and hassle of being kept in a shop environment.

Pet shops have a large selection of cages and all the other equipment that you will need. So, by visiting the pet shop you can get your cockatiel and everything you need to look after it.

Ask an adult to help you look up cockatiel breeders in your neighbourhood.

Male or female?

If you have decided to get just one cockatiel, you need to decide whether to have a male or a female bird. There are slight differences in colouring between the sexes, but not much in terms of **temperament** and intelligence, and both sexes make equally good pets. Obviously, if you buy a male and female pair, they may have babies! So if you are not ready for this, make sure you buy either just one bird, or two of the same sex.

How can you tell?

The **variation** in colouring between the sexes is the easiest way to be sure of telling what sex your bird is, but this is not noticeable until the bird is several months old. If you are getting a young bird the pet shop or breeder should probably be able to tell you which sex the bird is before you buy it.

Males usually have stronger, brighter colours than females, especially in the cheek patches.

You should have a good look around the shop before you buy your pet.

Hand-reared or not hand-reared?

A hand-reared bird is one that has been fed and handled by humans from an early age. These can either be bought direct from a breeder or from some good pet shops. Hand-reared birds will be pretty tame right from the start, which will save you the time of having to get them used to human contact. On the down side hand-reared cockatiels will cost a lot more money (maybe three or four times as much) than a bird that wasn't hand-reared. If you are planning to get a young bird and have plenty of time to spend taming it yourself, it won't be long before your new pet is as tame as a hand-reared one.

Top tip

Pet rescue centres sometimes have older birds that are already tame. They will be in need of a new home, and will be cheaper to buy than other hand-reared birds.

These 10-day old chicks are being hand fed by a breeder.

How will I know if it is healthy?

When you go to choose your new pet there are a few things that you need to look out for that will show you if the bird is healthy and likely to make a good pet.

The first thing to check for is the smell. Although birds will give off a faint bird **aroma** there shouldn't be any bad smells. Droppings will naturally be seen on the floor of the cage, but there shouldn't be a thick covering all over the perches. If the breeder or pet shop owner is looking after them properly and they are healthy, the cockatiel cages should be reasonably clean and not smelly.

Cockatiels sleep when it gets dark, so if you go to choose your new pet during the day when it is light, the birds should all be awake. They should be feeding or flying around. A sleepy bird may have a doze on its perch with one leg tucked up under itself, but it will soon straighten up and open its eyes when you move closer.

What age?

If you want to tame your cockatiel it is best to get one as young as possible, as soon as it is ready to leave its mother. This will be at around 8-12 weeks. Older birds will also make excellent pets, but will probably take longer to tame.

This young cockatiel is ideal to keep as a pet as it will take less time to become tame.

18

Watch out

If a bird is sitting with its eyes closed and its feathers all puffed up and does not respond when you get closer, it is probably best to choose another one. A healthy bird will be **alert** and lively. It will be friendly, but a bit nervous.

You should also pay attention to the condition of the feathers. Although the odd one or two may have been pulled out during fights with other birds in their cage, a healthy cockatiel will always make sure that its feathers are kept clean.

You should look closely when choosing your bird and compare how it looks with the others in the cage.

Top tip

If you can get a closer look, make sure that there is no **discharge** coming from the bird's eyes, beak, beak **vents** or bottom. A bird with runny eyes or beak or with droppings stuck all round its bottom, should be avoided.

What do I need?

The first thing that you will need to buy before you get your new cockatiel is a nice cage, and the bigger the better. For a single bird the cage shouldn't be any smaller than 60 cm × 60 cm × 90 cm. A pair of birds should ideally be given twice as much space. Cockatiels like to climb up and down, and in the wild they would naturally spend much of their time on the ground looking for food and then fly up into the trees. So, if you have the choice, it is better to get a tall cage than a wide one of the same size.

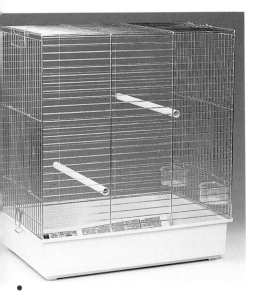

Cockatiels are climbers and will enjoy exploring the cage on foot. The bars of the cage should therefore be horizontal so that they can use them as a ladder. You should make sure that the bars of the cage are not more than 1 centimetre apart, otherwise your new pet may push its head through the bars and hurt itself.

You should also make sure that the cage is 'chew-proof' as your new bird will manage to bite its way through most plastics and wood if given enough time.

There are plenty of metal cages designed especially for cockatiels that are a good size and made of the right materials.

20

Top tip

Some cages, particularly antique ones, come in a wide variety of shapes and colours and even shiny metal. These may look nice, but can be very dangerous for your cockatiel. The paint used to make these designer cages can be poisonous to birds, so you should avoid these and stick to the ones sold at good pet shops.

Fitting out the cage

Once you have the main cage, you will need to add some perches. It is a good idea to put a few in at different angles and at different heights to represent the branches of trees that they would explore in the wild. It is very important to include perches of different thicknesses; this will help to exercise the bird's feet by getting it to grip different sized bars.

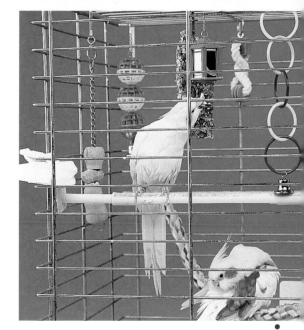

The bottom of the cage should be lined with a suitable covering especially for bird cages. These can be bought from most good pet shops. You can buy sheets of **grit**-covered paper that can be thrown away each day once they become covered in droppings. Or you can use special bird-friendly wood shavings. These are slightly more difficult to clean out and replace but only need to be done every couple of days.

Always make sure that there is enough room between the perches for your cockatiel to fly and stretch its wings.

Some cockatiels have a bad reaction to the ink used in newsprint. Check with your vet about the best lining material.

Inside or outside?

The 'indoor or outdoor' question very much depends on how much space you have in your home and how many birds you wish to keep. Normally a single bird or a pair of birds would be kept in a cage in the house, though you could keep them outside if necessary.

An outside cage or aviary usually allows you to give the birds more space but it will require a great deal of time and effort to make.

An outside cage will also have to meet a lot of special requirements to ensure that the bird is kept safe, well and happy. Unless you intend to keep several birds, or you simply do not have space in your home, start off with a single bird or a pair of birds kept in the house. This will enable you to spend much more time with them. They will also become **tamer** as they will live as part of your family on a daily basis.

Travel cages

There may come a time when you will need to move your pet from one place to another, for example if you go on holiday and need to leave your pet with a friend, or if you need to take it to the vet. It is therefore a good idea to have a smaller travel cage that you keep for this purpose.

22

Toys

Cockatiels are very intelligent birds and need a lot of things to keep them busy and occupied. Although toys are no substitute for your company, they will help to keep your pet happy and entertained when you have other things to do.

There are a huge variety of toys specially designed for cockatiels and parrots that you can get from most good pet shops. The best ones are those that reflect the natural behaviour of the birds in the wild. Toys that allow your pet to climb will be particularly popular, as will toys made from ropes that can be picked at and slowly destroyed! Give your pet plenty of variety to stop it getting bored.

Some toys can be attached to the side of the cage while others can be left loose on the bottom.

Maybe you could set up the travel cage as a play cage so that your cockatiel is used to it and won't be scared if it has to be taken somewhere in it.

Food and water bowls

Most good cages will come complete with all the necessary bowls and containers for food and water. If not you will be able to buy them separately from most pet shops.

Make sure that the bowls are made out of a strong, chew-proof material and that they don't have any sharp edges that could hurt your pet.

Cuttlebones

A cuttlebone is the skeleton of a **cuttlefish**, which is rather like a **squid**. The cuttlebone is often seen in bird cages, and is flat, white, and looks like a plate. They have two main uses. Firstly, the cuttlebone is an excellent source of **calcium**, which your bird needs to help keep its bones and feathers healthy. Secondly, the cuttlebone is very hard and your cockatiel will chew it, and this helps to keep its beak in good condition and stops it from growing too long.

Grit

Cockatiels do not have the same way of eating and **digesting** food as we do. They need to swallow little bits of grit that stay inside them and help crush up the food, rather than chewing their food first like we would. They don't need to swallow a lot of grit, but some should always be available for them. You should replace the grit when it becomes old or covered in droppings, but one small bag will be more than enough to last your bird its whole life.

You can buy special bird grit from most good pet shops and it should be offered to your bird in a separate container from the food.

This cockatiel is chewing on a cuttlebone. Remember to replace the cuttlebones when they get eaten.

Caring for your cockatiel

Once you have set up the cage with all the correct equipment and bought your new pet, you can start to get to know each other. The best way to do this is to spend as much time with it as possible. Soon you will have settled into a routine that works for both of you, and enables you to give your cockatiel the best care possible.

The living room is probably the best place for the cage, or even your bedroom if you spend a lot of time there.

Where should I put the cage?

Since cockatiels are such friendly birds and love plenty of attention, it is best to put the cage in a room that gets used a lot. Although the kitchen may be the busiest room the smells and sounds from the cooking may be a bit too much for your new pet. In fact, some smells may even be harmful.

Top tip

- You need to make sure that the cage is not in a **draught**, so not right by the door or window.
- It is also much better to put the cage higher up. This will keep your bird out of the way of any other household pets and give it a better view of what is going on in the house.

Once your cockatiel becomes tame you can bring it out of its cage to play with it.

Never leave your pet in its cage outside on its own as visiting cats or dogs from the neighbourhood could come over and scare it.

Taking your cockatiel outside

Even a very **tame** bird should never be taken outside without being in a cage. The most well-behaved bird can become confused outside, fly off and not be able to find its way back home. However, your bird will enjoy being taken outside in its cage to get a bit of fresh air and a change of scenery. Make sure that you don't put the cage

in direct sunlight. Even if part of the cage is in the sun there should always be a part in the shade, too, where your bird can go if it gets too hot. Also make sure that it's not raining or very cold as your pet won't like this.

27

What should I feed my cockatiel?

A cockatiel should be fed roughly 50% cereals, grains and seeds, 45% fresh vegetables and 5% fresh fruit. There are plenty of ready-made bird feeds that contain just the right things and will save you a huge amount of time and effort.

You can then add fresh fruit and vegetables to give your bird a bit more variety. Oranges, apples, carrots, sprouts, spinach, broccoli and dandelions will all be very well received. A small slice of apple and a small sprout, for example, will be plenty for one day. Make sure you don't give them much more than this otherwise they may suffer from **diarrhoea**.

There are many different varieties of ready-made bird food available, so always read the labels to check that they are especially good for cockatiels.

Top tips

- You should always throw away any fresh food that is not eaten within one day. Any uneaten seeds can be left for a couple of days before you throw them out.
- Water should be replaced every day.

New food

If you introduce any new foods to your cockatiel, take special notice of your bird's health. If it seems to be having a bad reaction to the new food, like heavy breathing, runny droppings or drinking a lot of water, you should stop feeding it the new food at once.

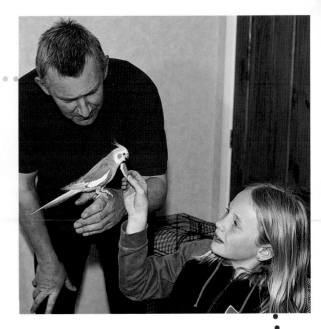

Be careful when you feed your pet new food.

Illness and injury

Cockatiels are not normally ill, but occasionally they may get the odd illness or injury. Watch how your pet normally looks and behaves so that you will be able to notice easily if it starts behaving differently, or showing signs of illness or injury. If you think that your cockatiel may be unwell or injured it is best to get a good vet to take a look at it.

Always remember to wash your hands before and after you handle your bird or the cage.

Cleaning out the cage

As well as the daily and weekly jobs of cleaning the floor of the cage, and the perches and toys, the whole cage will need to be cleaned out completely at least once a month. It is best to do this with someone to help, so that one of you can play with the bird or supervise it flying around the room while the other cleans out the cage.

Getting into a routine

It is a good idea with any pet to get into a routine that suits you. If you always get up at 8:00 a.m. but are too rushed and tired to spend time with your pet, get them used to just being given a quick bit of food at this time. When you get home in the evening and have more time to spend with your pet, you can give them their main feed, clean out the cage and play with them. They will soon get used to this routine and will be ready waiting for you in the evening, knowing that it is their time.

Top Tip

If your bird is not so tame or you don't have anyone to help you, you should buy a second cage that your bird can wait in until its normal cage is ready. Putting some special toys in the spare cage will help to keep your bird happy and amused.

Don't forget to clean under the cage, too. Cockatiels can be pretty messy!

Daily, weekly and monthly tasks

Every day you should:
- give your pet fresh food and water
- throw away any uneaten food from the day before
- change the flooring of the cage
- give your pet plenty of exercise flying around the room (as long as it is safe to do so)
- spend as much time playing with your pet as possible.

Once a week you should:
- clean the perches, toys and bowls
- give your pet a wash! (see page 36).

Once a month you should:
- clean out the whole cage with a good pet cage **disinfectant**.

Too busy to look after your cockatiel

A tame cockatiel will be unhappy if you leave it on its own for more than about eight hours a day. Leaving the TV or radio on will help to keep your pet happy, but this can't be done every day. You should aim to spend at least an hour a day playing and talking with your pet. The rest of the time it should be able to **interact** with your family, watching you all go about your daily tasks.

Placing a mirror in the cage will also help to keep your pet occupied.

Can we make friends?

As we have already discussed, a single cockatiel kept as a pet will be a lot easier to **tame** than a pair or a whole **aviary** full, and getting a **hand-reared** bird will also make the taming process a lot easier. The main thing to remember is that the more time you spend with your cockatiel, the tamer it will become.

Once you bring your new pet home, you should give it a few hours of peace and quiet just to settle into its new home. You will probably be very excited and keen to start getting to know it as soon as possible, but it will be quite nervous at first so give it some time on its own before you start.

Winning your cockatiel's trust

Once your cockatiel gets used to its new cage you could start by offering it a tasty treat through the bars of the cage (such as a bit of cabbage or apple) whilst speaking to it in a gentle, quiet voice. Once it is happy to come and take the food from your fingers, you can try putting your hand inside the cage to offer the treats. This may take a few days.

Eventually, your new pet will happily come and sit on your finger as soon as you put your hand inside the cage.

Be very patient when you are first making friends with your new pet.

Out of the cage

If the room is safe, and all doors and windows are closed, you can gently bring your finger, with your bird perched on it, out of the cage.

It will take a while to build up the relationship between you and your cockatiel, but they are quick learners, and if you spend enough time with them, (especially in the first few months) they will become very tame.

If you press your finger gently on your cockatiels chest, as if offering it as a perch, your bird will naturally climb up on to it. This is how you can return your tame cockatiel to its cage once its playtime is over.

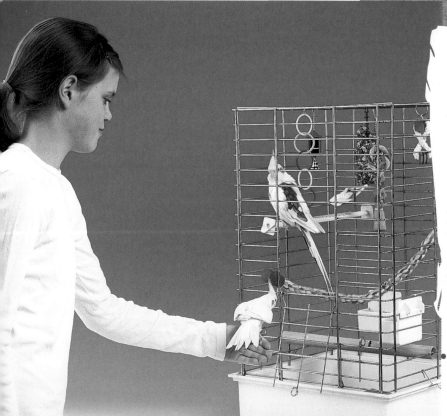

Fun time together

Because cockatiels are so intelligent and eager to learn, they can quite easily be taught to do simple tricks. Putting a coin in a purse or a toy in a toy box are the sort of tricks that your cockatiel will quickly learn and enjoy doing.

The easiest way to teach your cockatiel this sort of trick is with **bribery**! If you put a shiny new coin on the table in front of your bird it should naturally pick it up out of curiosity, to see what it is. You should then give your bird a little treat. A nice slice of apple or a piece of cabbage is a good choice.

Next time, offer the treat once the coin is picked up but from a little distance away, making the bird walk a few paces to get the treat. Once it gets to the treat still carrying the coin, the treat can be given. Continue to do this in stages until the bird understands that it only gets the treat if it picks up and carries the coin to you. You can then introduce the purse and follow the same steps.

Once your cockatiel is tame you can teach it lots of fun tricks!

This is the basic way to teach a cockatiel to do things, slowly and in simple stages. You can be as imaginative as you like and teach your cockatiel to do all sorts of entertaining tricks, which will be great fun for you and your pet.

An adventure playground

Cockatiels love to climb and explore and they love nothing better than to be let loose on an interesting selection of safe, objects they can chew! Old kitchen roll tubes, cardboard boxes (without any print), ropes and other similar things you can think of, will all be gratefully received. You can really use your imagination and create a fantastic adventure playground for your pet. You will have a lot of fun building it and your cockatiel will have hours of pleasure destroying it!

Top tip

Make sure that the adventure playground is set up in a safe place and never leave your bird on its own when it is out of its cage. Even the seemingly harmless places can have hidden dangers for your pet.

Ladders, swings and climbing frames will keep your cockatiel entertained.

Having a bath

Cockatiels like to look their best and so will be very happy if you offer them a bath. You can let them use a large shallow dish filled with a few millimetres of clean water. If you choose to do this, make sure you supervise your pet at all times when it is using the bath in case it drowns. Don't leave the dish of water in the cage. Remove it when your bird has finished.

The other way of cleaning your cockatiel is to spray it with water from a clean spray bottle.

Always make sure that the spray bottle is completely clean and has never contained any chemicals that may be harmful to your bird.

You can offer your bird a bath in a specially-made cockatiel bath!

Catching a cold

Never leave a wet cockatiel outside or in a **draught**, as it will easily catch a cold. After your cockatiel has washed, make sure that there is somewhere warm where it can sit to dry off. Never try to dry it with a hair dryer!

Teaching your cockatiel to talk

Cockatiels are not great talkers in comparison to some of the larger parrots or even budgies. However, if you have the patience, a cockatiel should be able to learn a few words. You should repeat the same word over and over again with a little gap in between, and spoken in the same tone of voice. Try not to be too ambitious – start with its name or 'Hello', and once that has been learnt and happily repeated, you can move on to other slightly longer phrases. Bribery will work here, too, so always keep a tasty bit of apple ready to reward your bird if it says things correctly.

Each bird's talking ability is very different and some may never utter a single word despite hours of patient teaching. But if your bird does learn to say a few things it will be well worth the effort.

Cockatiels may not be great talkers, but they are certainly great companions.

Keeping your cockatiel healthy

Cockatiels are normally very healthy birds and don't usually become sick. The best way to keep them healthy is to make sure they are well cared for.

Draughts are one of the main causes of illness in cockatiels. Cockatiels can catch a cold very easily, so to keep your pet healthy it should be kept out of draughts. Boredom is the other main problem and can lead to the death of a bird. If you keep your cockatiels in a draught-free, warm, dry, clean environment in a large cage, giving them fresh food and water every day and spending as much time with them as possible, you should have a very healthy bird.

Once you have had the new bird checked up by the vet you can put it in with the others and watch it make friends.

New bird

The only other situation that could be potentially dangerous for your pet is if a new bird is introduced to either a single bird or an **aviary**. The new bird could bring with it any number of diseases, as you will not be sure if it is completely healthy when you buy it. If you have decided to buy a second bird to keep your single bird company, or you wish to add another to your aviary, you must keep it separately until you have had it checked by a good veterinarian.

Wing, beak and claw clipping

Wing clipping is a difficult subject, some people like to do it and others are strongly against it. It basically means that some of the wing feathers are cut so that the bird can't fly away, which sometimes makes **taming** the bird easier. If you do wish to have your bird's wings clipped you should take it to a vet to get their help and advice. Never try to do it yourself as you could end up hurting your bird very badly.

Beak and claw clipping is a different matter altogether and is done to help improve the bird's health and quality of life. Beak clipping may need to be done in some birds where the beak has become overgrown and is stopping the bird from eating properly. Claws will need to be clipped if they become too long and are making it difficult for your bird to walk and hold on to its perches. However, never try to clip the beak or claws yourself as you can easily hurt your pet.

If you think that your bird's claws or beak have become too long, you should take it to a vet who will be able to clip them for you.

39

Some health problems

In the wild, birds that become ill will normally try to pretend that they are not. They will not want to seem unwell as this will attract the attention of **predators** who would see them as easy **prey**. Cockatiels that are kept as pets will also often hide the fact that they are not feeling well, which makes it difficult for you to tell if they are poorly.

A sick cockatiel will usually sit on the ground or at the end of a perch with its feathers all puffed up, eyes closed and its head tucked back. It won't seem very **alert** even if you talk to it and will generally not seem like its normal self.

Other signs of illness or injury include: runny droppings; runny eyes, beak or beak **vents**; breathing problems; messy feathers; a dirty bottom and a lack of interest in everything. If you think that your cockatiel is unwell or injured you should take it to the vet at once.

If your cockatiel looks puffed up it may just be sleepy or cold so make sure that is not the case before you take it to the vet.

Colds

As we have already learnt, cockatiels should never be kept in a **draught** as this can easily cause breathing problems and colds. If your bird starts to make wheezing noises and appears to be having trouble breathing you should keep it separate from any other birds and get it to a vet as soon as possible.

This is what healthy cockatiel droppings should look like.

Burns

Cockatiels don't automatically know if something is going to be hot. If you let your bird fly into the kitchen and the electric hob is on, your bird will simply see it as a nice flat landing surface and get bad burns on its feet.

Drowning

One fairly common cause of death in **tame** cockatiels is drowning. Half full glasses of wine or water will look very appealing to a cockatiel, but they can easily fall in and get stuck, head down in the liquid, drowning themselves in seconds.

Boredom

It is important not to let your cockatiel get bored. This is the most common cause of death in all parrots. If you feel that you are unable to give your bird the attention it needs, either find it a new home or get another cockatiel to keep it company.

A cockatiel should never be left alone with no company or toys to keep it busy.

When a cockatiel dies

Sadly, the time will come when your pet will die. This is obviously a very natural thing and there is nothing that you can do to stop it from happening. It doesn't matter how well you look after your pet, one day it will just be time for it to go. Sometimes this will happen without warning and you may discover your pet has passed away during the night. Other times you may be aware that your pet is sick or old and the vet may tell you that it will die very soon.

If your cockatiel is too ill or old to enjoy its life you and your vet may decide to put it to sleep.

Putting to sleep

Sometimes you and your vet may feel that a sick or very old cockatiel is no longer enjoying its life and that the kindest thing to do for it would be to 'put it to sleep'. The vet will simply give your pet a little injection, which won't hurt it at all, and it will very quickly fall into a nice deep sleep and its heart will just stop. It won't feel any pain and it will all be over very quickly. It is a very difficult decision to make, but it is also a very brave one, and one that shows that you are doing the best thing for your pet.

Feeling sad

When something that we love dies, it is a very difficult and sad time. It is important to understand that your pet didn't suffer in any way and that it died peacefully after a happy life. Death is just one of those things that happens and it is not your fault in any way.

It is normal for both children and adults to cry when a loved pet dies or when we think about a pet that has died. After a while the sadness will pass and you can just remember the good times that you had with your pet.

You can decorate the grave with flowers so that your pet's resting place looks very special.

43

Keeping a record

Just like any friend or member of your family, your pet should have a place in your photo album, or even an album all of its own. This will be fun to create and after your pet has died it will give you something to remember it by.

It is also a nice idea to make notes about your cockatiel, when you first brought it home and how you **tamed** it. Maybe you could keep a diary of all the things that you did with your pet and the progress it made as you tamed it and taught it new tricks.

Take photos of your bird with different members of your family and all your friends that come round, and create a 'hall of fame' with all the people that your bird played with. You can also take some pictures of your bird doing its favourite tricks and eating its favourite food. You could then make up funny captions to go with your pictures and set them out in a comic-style book about your pet.

You can have great fun, taking lots of pictures of your cockatiel doing all the things that you both enjoy.

A special diary

Why not keep a scrapbook full of cut-outs from magazines, and articles that you find about cockatiels and other parrots. You can really be creative, decorating it with lots of pictures and include some of your own drawings. You could even write your own book about keeping and caring for cockatiels!

Top tip

You can start your scrapbook with the first day you saw your pet and then go on to show how your friendship grew!

A scrapbook is a great way to record your pet's life and it will stay with you for years after you've said goodbye to it.

COCKATIEL

my pet Joey

Glossary

albino   white, without any colour at all

alert   aware of what is going on around it, lively

aroma   special smell

aviary   large cage for keeping birds in, normally kept outside

bribery   being offered something nice if you do what you are asked

calcium   element found in some foods that helps to keep bones healthy

camouflage   having a special shape, colour or pattern that helps a living thing go unnoticed by a predator or prey

crest   tuft of feathers on the head of a bird

cuttlefish   white flat bone of a squid-like creature

diarrhoea   runny droppings

digest   break up food that is eaten so that it can be used by the body

discharge   oozing liquid

disinfectant   special medicated cleaning liquid

draught   gust of air through an enclosed space

grit   very small bits of stone

guarantee   promise to do something

hand-reared   brought up by humans, not in the wild

hollows   holes

interact   talk to, play with

Portuguese   coming from Portugal

predator   animal that eats other animals

prey   animal that is eaten by a predator

rear   feed and care for from when it is a baby

rodents   small animals such as mice or rats with two long front teeth

squid   sea creature, bit like an octopus

stimulation   something to keep its interest

tame   used to being with people

temperament   its character, if it is friendly, moody, angry, etc.

variation   difference

vents   air holes

Useful addresses

RSPCA (London headquarters)
20 Station Road
South Norwood
London
SE25 2AJ
http://www.rspca.org.uk

There are several national organizations for cockatiel welfare, which all give helpful advice on caring for your cockatiel. They may also be able to help you find smaller local clubs and recommend well-qualified vets in your area.

UK
The Cockatiel Society
Secretary: Mr Michael O Hare
7 Moorlands
Wellingborough
Northants
NN8 5QS
Tel: 01933 673089

USA
The National Cockatiel Society
Secretary: Nancy Rocheleau
1828 Stovall Street
Bullhead City, AZ   86443
(928) 704-2883 (Ph/Fax)
nancyr10@citilink.net

Australia
The Native Cockatiel Society of Australia Inc
P.O. Box 6308
South Penrith, NSW 2750

More books to read

The Complete Book of Cockatiels, Diane Grindol (John Wiley and Sons Inc., 1998)
Cockatiels Today, Dennis Kelsey-Wood (TFH Publications, 1996)
Taming and Training Cockatiels, Risa Teitler (TFH Publications, 1995)

Helpful websites

http://www.theparrotsocietyuk.org/soc.htm
http://www.cockatiel.org
http://www.letstalkbirds.com/cockatiels.htm
http://www.cockatiel.com

Index